T0013846

Contents

Korimako
Bellbird
p 22

Kārearea
NZ Falcon
p 24

Pūkeko
p 20

Ruru
Morepork
p 18

Pīwakawaka
Fantail
p 2

Tūī
p 4

Kererū
NZ wood pigeon
p 12

Kiwi
p 28

Hihi
Stitchbird
p 14

Tīeke
Saddleback
p 6

Kōkako
p 8

Takahē
p 32

Whio
Blue Duck
p 10

NZ parrots
Kea, Kākā, Kākāpō
p 26

Extinct birds
Moa, Pouakai, Huia
p 30

SQUAWK!
DONOVAN BIXLEY'S
FOREST BIRDS OF AOTEAROA

A catalogue record for this book is available
from the National Library of New Zealand.

978-1-86971-456-7 (hardback)

Published in New Zealand in 2022
by Hachette Aotearoa New Zealand
(an imprint of Hachette New Zealand Limited)
Level 2, 23 O'Connell Street, Auckland, New Zealand
www.hachette.co.nz

Copyright © Donovan Bixley 2022
The moral rights of the illustrator have been asserted.

All rights reserved. No part of this publication may be
reproduced or transmitted in any form or by any means,
electronic or mechanical, including photocopying,
recording, or any information storage and retrieval system,
without the permission in writing from the publisher.

Cover and internal design by Donovan Bixley
Printed by 1010 Printing, China

MOA

Pīwakawaka FANTAIL

Has a small bird just flitted past you in the garden? Does it have a tail spread wide like a waving hand? Pīwakawaka are found all over Aotearoa — from the seaside to the mountains, and in towns as well as the countryside. Their fanned-out tail feathers make them easy to identify.

That big fan tail flicks open and closed. It helps pīwakawaka change direction quickly when they are flying. They can easily catch small bugs darting about in the air.

WHERE
● **PĪWAKAWAKA LIVE**

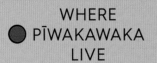

SIZE

Have you seen an all-black fantail? Lucky you! The black fantail is very rare. It sometimes has a white mark near its eye, but has no white markings on its tail.

Pīwakawaka are friendly birds. They love to follow bigger birds or people tramping through leafy bush. They dive down to snatch insects disturbed by trampers' feet. Fantails sometimes hang upside down in trees picking bugs from the underside of leaves.

Māori have more than twenty names for fantail, including tīwaiwaka and tīrairaka.

3

Tūī

If a black bird has just darted past, take a closer look. Although it may have looked black at first glance, tūī feathers shimmer blue and green in the sunlight. Tūī have special white feathers on their neck curled together to look like a ball.

Tūī like to sing. They know hundreds of songs. They can even copy the sound of a car alarm — annoying! There are some chirps a tūī makes that can't be heard by human ears.

These birds are so good at copying sounds that Māori used to teach pet tūī to talk.

Ka rawe!

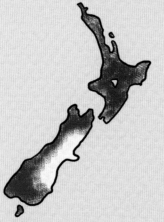

WHERE TŪĪ LIVE

2L MILK

SIZE

Tūī fly all over Aotearoa feeding on fruit and nectar from flowers, like this kōwhai.

Tūī are important to our environment because they pollinate plants, just like bees do.

Tīeke SADDLEBACK

What was that bird you spotted hopping between the branches? It looked like a common blackbird, but it had a red pouch under its beak. It could be a tīeke. They also have a unique brown patch on their back, which gives them their European name, saddleback.

Saddlebacks are not made for long flights. Instead they have strong legs and leap from branch to branch like a monkey, or spring about on the forest floor looking for food. This behaviour puts them in danger from animals on the ground like rats and stoats.

Yeehaw!

HEY!

Tīeke are so rare that you can only see them in protected reserves.

● WHERE TĪEKE LIVE

Tīeke belong to a special group called wattlebirds. Wattles are the distinctive fleshy pouch hanging down on either side of the beak.

In the myth of how Māui slowed the sun, cheeky tīeke refused to bring Māui water. So Māui grabbed tīeke with his hot hand leaving a scorched mark on the bird's back forever.

2L MILK

SIZE

The saddleback's beak is a powerful tool. It is used to hammer away at rotten bark and poke under leaves, like on this tī kōuka/cabbage tree, while looking for yummy insects.

Kōkako

What was that masked bird in the high forest branches? Was it a superhero or a supervillain? Kōkako has a black face mask and just like a masked villain, they can be hard to catch. They like to hide in tall native trees — but their long slow songs can be heard from far away.

The kōkako is a wattlebird, like the tīeke. The North Island kōkako has bright blue wattles. The South Island kōkako has orange wattles and was once thought extinct. It has been nicknamed 'the grey ghost' because it is so hard to find.

Phew!

In Māori legend, friendly kōkako brought Māui water to cool his thirst after he had slowed the sun — what a superhero!

● WHERE NORTH ISLAND KŌKAKO LIVE

South Island kōkako have been heard distantly in the forest, but not seen for many years.

2L MILK

SIZE

Like many of our birds, kōkako are endemic – that means they are found only in New Zealand. Not like me, I'm found all over the world! Baaaa!

Whio BLUE DUCK

Did you just see a duck riding the white water rapids in the river? You may have spotted a whio. They are the only New Zealand duck species who live all year round on fast-flowing rivers. Whio were once found all across Aotearoa. Now they are rarer than some species of kiwi.

SIZE

Whio are expert surfers. Even baby chicks can handle the rough water at just one day old! Whio use the rapids to evade predators by riding swiftly downstream and diving underwater when they are in danger. When they are safe they retreat to their roosts on the river's edge among caves or washed-up logs.

Whio have forward facing eyes, like us, and whio dads are very good lookouts. They will see you long before you see them and call out 'fee-oo fee-oo' as a warning to other birds.

Whio only like the best water, so if you see a pair and their chicks it means the river and plants are very healthy. Cool!

● WHERE WHIO LIVE

Kererū NZ WOOD PIGEON

Did you hear a slow 'woop-woop-woop' of a bird passing overhead? Look around. It may have settled on a nearby tree. If you see a plump green bird who looks as if it's wearing a white singlet, you've spotted a kererū.

Kererū are our largest pigeon. They are also the only pigeon native to Aotearoa. Kererū like to party — feasting on native fruit, flowers and leaves. If they eat too much sweet fruit they get giddy. Sometimes they fall right off their branches!

2L MILK

SIZE COMPARED TO
A COMMON PIGEON

⬤ WHERE KERERŪ LIVE

But it's not all party time. We have important work to do in our forests.

Since giant moa became extinct hundreds of years ago, only kererū are big enough to eat the large fruit of trees like karaka, miro and tawa.

Just doing my job.

pfft

Kererū help spread native trees, like this kahikatea (our tallest trees), by pooping seeds across the country.

13

Hihi STITCHBIRD

Did you catch that bright dash of yellow zipping through the green bush? Good spotting! Hihi are hard to find. They are one of the rarest birds in Aotearoa. Female hihi are olive brown making them even harder to spot. The flashy males have yellow and black feathers with spiky tufts that flick up and make them look like punk rockers.

Hihi are curious birds and will flutter close to people to check them out. While adult birds are away searching for food, chicks from different nests like to get together and play.

In Māori 'hihi' also means the gleaming rays of sunlight. The hihi bird carries the sun's yellow markings on its shoulders, spreading a healing glow throughout the forest.

2L MILK

SIZE

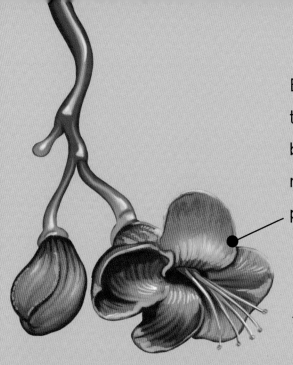

Being small, hihi avoid the tree tops where bigger birds like tūī bully them out of food. Hihi eat nectar from blossoms like this pūriri flower.

WHERE HIHI LIVE

Hihi are only found in protected areas. They are very sensitive to changes in the forest. If you see hihi, it means that the forest is thriving with native wildlife.

Ruru MOREPORK

Did you hear that hoot of 'more-pork, more-pork' in the dark? The sad call of the ruru can be heard all over Aotearoa and gives them their European name, morepork. Sometimes ruru can be seen during the day roosting in holes in trees or on top of a ponga fern, but night-time is when they really come out to play.

Like other owls, ruru have big eyes that allow them to see in the dark. Their eyes also face forward, helping to pinpoint insects like this huhu beetle.

For Māori, the call of 'more-pork' in the dark forest was a good sign. But if a ruru made a high pitched 'yelp', it was thought to be a warning ... eeek looks like I'm in trouble!

WHERE RURU LIVE

2L MILK

SIZE

Ruru have a secret weapon on their night-time hunts. They have special feathers on their wing edges. These feathers reduce the sound of their flapping wings as they swoop down silently on their prey.

Ruru are native to New Zealand, but they are not endemic — they are also found in Tasmania, Australia.

Crikey!

Pūkeko

Whoosh! Did you see that blue bird with a chunky red beak as you zoomed past in the car? Pūkeko are one of our most common birds. You often see them stalking along roadsides near waterways and swamplands.

Pūkeko are bold and cheeky, often digging up garden vegetables and stealing fruit.

SIZE

With long legs and oversized feet, pūkeko look like goofy clowns when they run but are perfectly adapted for walking on swampy marshes. Even though they don't have webbed feet, pūkeko are also great swimmers.

Unlike many of our native birds, pūkeko live happily near humans and introduced animals. They are found all over Aotearoa New Zealand.

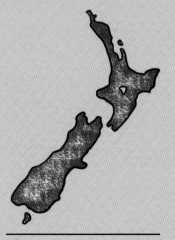

● WHERE PŪKEKO
   LIVE

If attacked, a pūkeko will usually run away rather than fly. Pūkeko look clumsy when flying but they can travel long distances. It is thought that the first group of pūkeko to arrive in Aotearoa flew all the way from Australia about a thousand years ago.

Korimako BELLBIRD

Who was whistling that bubbly song? It sounded like someone blowing on a toy water whistle in the bathtub. Korimako are so famous for their beautiful singing that Māori compare great singers to the voice of the bellbird.

Like tūī and hihi, korimako feed from flowers. They have a special tongue, with a tip like the bristles of a paint brush, to lap up the sweet nectar.

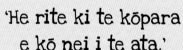

'He rite ki te kōpara e kō nei i te ata.'

'Just like a bellbird singing at dawn.'

2L MILK

SIZE

The bellbird is also called kōpara, makomako or komako. They like berries such as these from the kaikomako tree. Kai komako means 'food for the komako'.

Korimako spread seeds and pollen. This helps our native plants to thrive across Aotearoa.

● WHERE KORIMAKO LIVE

23

Kārearea NZ FALCON

Did you see a winged blur plummet from the sky before snatching its prey from the air? Kārearea are master hunters and even catch prey bigger than themselves. They can fly at 100km per hour — that's as fast as a car!

When hunting, kārearea dive out of tall trees. Their large tail helps them twist and turn quickly between branches as they swoop down on their prey. They prefer to hunt live animals, so if you see a large bird scavenging on the side of the highway it's probably a kahu (Australasian hawk), and not a kārearea.

Kārearea don't build nests. They usually scrape a shallow hole on the ground for their eggs.

They will defend their chicks like a great warrior.

SIZE

2L MILK

Kārearea have unique dark feathers under their beak, which look like a droopy moustache.

Unlike the hawk, kārearea are found only in Aotearoa, but they are much harder to spot. They are equally happy to live in pine trees or native forests.

● WHERE KĀREAREA LIVE

25

NZ Parrots

KEA

Oh no! Who broke the car mirror? If your car was parked in the snowy mountains of the South Island, the vandal was probably a kea. Kea are one of the smartest animals in the world. They can unlock complicated puzzles to get at food. Flying is playtime for kea, and they love doing acrobatic twirls as much as they love causing mischief.

New Zealand's parrots are world famous. The kea is the only parrot to live in snowy mountains, and the kākāpō is the world's largest parrot.

KĀKĀ

Kākā look very similar to kea, but are not as naughty. Kākā like the native forest across Aotearoa, but they can also be seen in big cities. Sometimes kākā get together for a big party, chatting away noisily, but when they are alone they are so quiet you'd hardly know they were near.

Kākāpō are one of the strangest parrots in the world. As well as being the heaviest, they are also the only flightless parrot. They are great climbers and can reach the top of the tallest trees searching for berries and seeds. Kākāpō feathers are the perfect colour for hiding in the forest. Long ago, kākāpō became nocturnal — only active at night-time — to avoid predators like the giant eagle, pouakai.

KĀKĀPŌ

To be a parrot you must have zygodactyl feet like mine - with two claws facing forward and two backward.

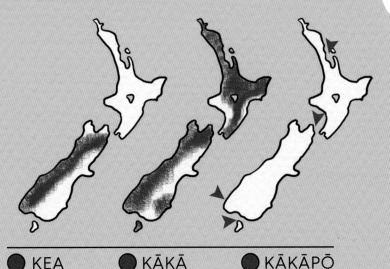

● KEA   ● KĀKĀ   ● KĀKĀPŌ

KĀKĀPŌ

KEA AND KĀKĀ

2L MILK

SIZE COMPARISON

Kiwi

Look at that bird with the long bill. It's impossible to mistake a kiwi for any other animal. Its long bill is not the only amazing thing about the kiwi; they are nocturnal, like kākāpō, and have whiskers like a cat for night-time foraging. Kiwi spend up to six hours a night looking for bugs and native berries.

Kiwi have tiny wings that you can't see. Their feathers are not made for flying. They are like fern fronds and hang like shaggy hair for warmth. Being flightless, kiwi have powerful legs with razor sharp claws for digging burrows or fighting enemies. Most birds have light bones for flying, but kiwi bones are thick and heavy.

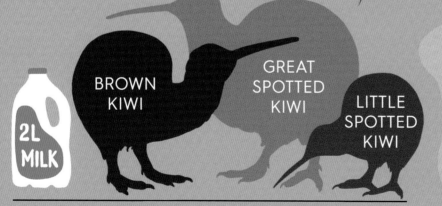

2L MILK

BROWN KIWI

GREAT SPOTTED KIWI

LITTLE SPOTTED KIWI

SIZE COMPARISON

There are three main types of kiwi. The rarest and smallest is the little spotted kiwi, or pukupuku.

Unlike most birds, kiwi have no colour vision. Luckily we have a great sense of smell with special nostrils at the tip of our bill to help us find food.

Beaks are measured from the nostril to the tip. So kiwi have a long bill, but a short beak.

What a whopper! Compared to its body size, the female kiwi lays the largest eggs of any bird in the world. No wonder the mums are much bigger than the dads!

● WHERE KIWI LIVE

Extinct Birds

Some of our most impressive birds no longer exist. You will only see models of them or their bones in a museum. Moa are famous around the world as one of the largest birds to have ever lived. The tallest were as high as a netball goal post when they stood up straight.

Unlike other big flightless birds, such as emu and ostrich, moa had no wings. They used their long neck to graze plants for leaves and berries.

MOA

There were **nine** different types of moa. The smallest was the size of a turkey and biggest was heavier than three grown men — now that would make a big feast!

GIANT MOA

POUAKAI

SIZE COMPARISON

HUIA

Wow, you're gigantic!

POUAKAI

Pouakai, or Haast's Eagle, was the world's largest eagle. They fed on giant moa, swooping down with massive wings as long as a car and talons as big as a tiger's claw.

Huia were wattlebirds like kōkako, but a little bigger. They had beautiful tail feathers prized by Māori. Huia were one of the few birds in the world where the female and male have very different shaped beaks.

MALE HUIA

FEMALE HUIA

Extinct means that there are no longer any of these birds alive today – just like us dinosaurs.

These wonderful birds all became extinct as a result of humans hunting them or destroying their habitats.

Takahē

Did you see that huge blue bird? It looked as if it had eaten a football! Takahē have similar colours to the common pūkeko but they are so rare you won't see a takahē near the side of the highway.

For a long time takahē were thought to be extinct, like the moa. Amazingly, a small group were found on the South Island, where they eat tussock grass.

Takahē have a special sharp claw in their wings to help defend themselves. This is very useful as takahē cannot fly. They also use their large chomping beak and thick legs to chase off enemies.

● WHERE TAKAHĒ LIVE

SIZE

2L MILK

The survival of the takahē is a great success story. It shows that with care and protection all our native birds can thrive.

Which New Zealand
bird do you love
the most?